love

Flood waters can't drown love,

torrents of rain can't put it out.

Love can't be bought, love can't be sold—

it's not to be found in the marketplace.

SONG OF SOLOMON 8:7 THE MESSAGE

_____

Presented to

_____

Presented by

_____

Date

$\mathcal{Love}$ isn't like a reservoir.

You'll never drain it dry.

It's much more like a natural spring.

The longer and farther it flows,

the stronger and deeper and clearer it becomes.

EDDIE CANTOR

With all my love

A Keepsake of Quotes, Poems, and
Inspiration in Celebration of our Lives Together

Whoever *loves* true life,
will love true love.

ELIZABETH BARRETT BROWNING

If we love each other, God lives in
us, and his love has been brought to
full expression through us.

1 JOHN 4:12 NLT

tender hearted

Are your hearts tender and sympathetic?

Then make me truly happy by agreeing

wholeheartedly with each other,

loving one another, and working together

with one heart and purpose.

PHILIPPIANS 2:1–2 NLT

Be kind and compassionate to one another,
forgiving each other, just as in Christ God
forgave you.

EPHESIANS 4:32 NIV

The *kindest* and the *happiest* pair

Will find occasion to forbear;

And something, every day they live,

To pity and perhaps *forgive*.

WILLIAM COWPER

your unfailing

May your unfailing love rest upon us, O LORD,
even as we put our hope in you.

PSALM 33:22 NIV

love

Love is the thing

that enables a woman to sing

while she mops up the floor

after her husband

has walked across it in his barn boots.

HOOSIER FARMER

it must be love

what beauty

Ask not of me, love, what is *love*?

Ask what is good of God above—

Ask of the great sun what is light—

Ask sin of what may be forgiven—

Ask what is happiness of Heaven—

Ask what is folly of the crowd—

Ask what is fashion of the shroud—

Ask what is sweetness of thy kiss—

Ask of thyself what *beauty* is.

PHILIP JAMES BAILEY

In *real love* you want
the other person's good.

MARGARET ANDERSON

real love

Stand firm in the Lord's strength.
I love you and long for you.

PHILIPPIANS 4:1 NIrV

Let us *love* one another,

for love comes from God.

Everyone who loves has been born of God

and knows God.

1 JOHN 4:7 NIV

love gives

Love gives without thought of return.

ANDREA GARNEY

[God] didn't love in order to get something
from us, but to give everything of himself to us.
Love like that.

EPHESIANS 5:2 THE MESSAGE

May the Lord make your *love* increase

and overflow for each other

and for everyone else.

1 THESSALONIANS 3:12 NIV

you have

my heart

The most *precious* possession

that ever comes to a man

in this world is

a woman's *heart*.

JOSIAH G. HOLLAND

without love

Without *love*, hope perishes.

CHARLES R. SWINDOLL

Love bears all things,

believes all things,

hopes all things,

endures all things.

1 CORINTHIANS 13:7 NKJV

Let me give you my *hand*;

    May it ever be there for you.

Let me give you my *shoulder*;

    May it always comfort you.

Let me give you my *arms*;

    May they only hold you.

Let me give you my *heart*;

    May it only love you.

your hand

With *love* there is no cold, for each
provides *warmth*
for the other.

On a cold night, two under the same blanket

can gain warmth from each other.

But how can one be warm alone?

ECCLESIASTES 4:1 NLT

warmth

Love is the doorway

through which the

human soul passes

from selfishness to service

and from solitude

to kinship with

all mankind.

enter love!

Love always seeks to help,

never to hurt.

Who can find a virtuous wife? . . .
The heart of her husband safely trusts her.

PROVERBS 31:10–11 NKJV

There is no fear in *love*.

Instead, perfect love drives fear away.

Fear has to do with being punished.

The one who fears does not have *perfect love*.

1 John 4:18 NIrV

When I have learnt
to *love* God better
than my earthly dearest,
I shall *love* my earthly dearest
better than I do now.

C. S. LEWIS

Greet one another with a kiss of love.

1 PETER 5:14 NIV

Four *sweet* lips,

two *pure* souls, and

one undying affection—these are

love's pretty ingredients

for a *kiss*.

CHRISTIAN NESTELL BOVEE

Two persons who have chosen each other
out of all the species, with the design to
be each other's mutual *comfort* and
entertainment, have, in that action,
bound themselves to be good-humored,
affable, discreet, *forgiving*, patient,
and *joyful*, with respect to each other's frailties
and perfections, to the end of their *lives*.

JOSEPH ADDISON

soul mates

Love does not consist in

gazing at each other

but in looking together

in the same direction.

ANTOINE DE SAINT-EXUPÉRY

Agree with one another so that there may be
no divisions among you and that you may be
perfectly united in mind and thought.

1 CORINTHIANS 1:10 NIV

companion

Two are better than one,

Because they have a good reward

for their labor.

For if they fall, one will lift

up his companion.

ECCLESIASTES 4:9–10 NKJV

No *cord* nor cable

can so forcibly draw,

or hold so fast,

as *love* can do

with a twined thread.

ROBERT BURTON

hold me

A threefold cord is not quickly broken.

ECCLESIASTES 4:12 NKJV

close

intensely

See to it that you really do
love each other *intensely*
with all your hearts.

1 PETER 1:22 NLT

I love you,
not only for what you are,
but for what *I am*
when I am *with you.*

ROY CROFT

Your life is a journey you must travel with a
deep consciousness of God.

1 PETER 1:17 THE MESSAGE

life together

Love is what you've been
through together.

JAMES THURBER

Nothing is *sweeter* than *Love*,

Nothing is *stronger*,

Nothing *higher*,

Nothing *wider*,

Nothing more *pleasant*,

Nothing fuller nor better in heaven and earth.

THOMAS À KEMPIS

With All My Love
ISBN 1-40372-022-3

Published in 2005 by Spirit Press, an imprint of Dalmatian Press, LLC.
Copyright © 2005 Dalmatian Press, LLC. Franklin, Tennessee 37067.

Editor: Lila Empson
Compiler: Snapdragon Editorial Group, Inc., Tulsa, Oklahoma
Design: Diane Whisner, Tulsa, Oklahoma

Printed in China

05 06 07 LPU 10 9 8 7 6 5 4 3 2 1

SPIRIT PRESS